BLOOM
Founded by | arihant



# Olympiad ACE

## A Comprehensive Practice Book
for School Olympiads & Talent Search Exams

# SCIENCE
Class 1

by
Akriti Verma

**Olympiad ACE**

BLOOM

Bloom Cap Edu Ventures Pvt. Ltd.



**Administrative & Production Office**

'Ramchhaya' 4577/15, Agarwal Road, Darya Ganj, New Delhi -110002
Tele: 011- 47630600, 43518550

**PRICE:** ₹125.00

Published by Arihant Publications (I) Ltd.

For further information about the books log on to
www.bloomcap.org

Follow us on

# Preface

*"Future belongs to those Who prepares for it today"*

School Olympiads are National & International level competitions conducted by different Government, Non-Government & Educational Organisations with the purpose of making the children ready to face competitive exams.

The challenging Questions asked in Olympiads motivate them to learn more & more and bring out the best result with improved academic performance. The Awards & Scholarship offered by Olympiads motivate children to aspire & strive for doing better and emerge out to be the best.

## Science Olympiads

Being a Scientist or Engineer or Doctor has always been a dream of each school going child. A good command over Science is a must for any of these. Questions of Science Olympiads are structured to help students to develop scientific temperament & motivate them to understand the concepts of science. They also focuses on improving existing knowledge of a student by adding more information.

**'Bloom Science Olympiad Study Book Class 1'** is a perfect resource to Study & Practice for Olympiad Exams and other National & State Level Talent Search Exams & Other Competitions.

### Some Special Features of Bloom Science Olympiad Study Books are;

- Chapterwise Exercises having different types of Objective Questions; Analytical, Applications, Remembering etc, at par with the Olympiad Level.
- Detailed Explanation for each question.
- Olympiad Pattern Practice Sets at the end.

This book is prepared by Expert Panel with the utmost care, still if you have any suggestions regarding its improvement then feel free to contact us at support@bloomcap.org. We will try to inculcate your suggestions in the further editions.

# Contents

Chapter 01

# Living and Non-living Things

- There are many things around us. We can divide things on the basis of their features into living and non-living things.

**Things**

**Living**

Living things are those, who can breathe and move on their own natural, e.g. Dog, human, cow and plants.

**Non-living**

Non-living things are those, who cannot breathe and grow, e.g. Stone, fridge, water.

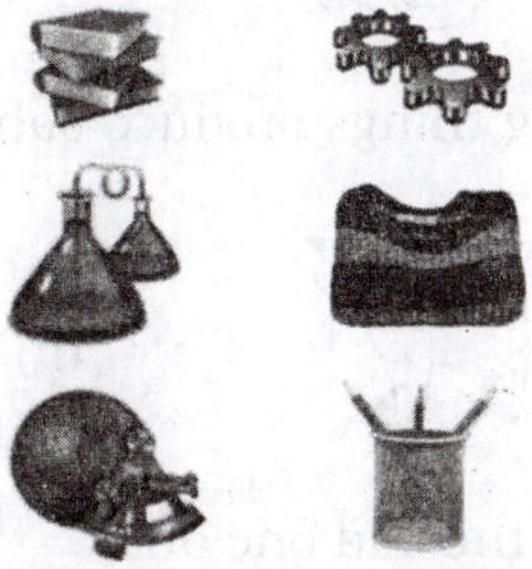

- We can differentiate living things and non-living things on the basis of following features.

| Things \ Features | Breathe | Move on their own | Need food and water | Feel | Reproduce | Grow |
|---|---|---|---|---|---|---|
| Living things | Yes | Yes | Yes | Yes | Yes | Yes |
| Non-living things | No | No | No | No | No | No |

- Non-living things are natural as well as man-made.
- Natural non-living things are rock, soil, water, etc.
- Man-made non-living things are fridge, fan, bat, eraser, etc.

# Let's Practice

1. Identify the non-living thing.

(a)  (b)  (c)  (d) 

2. Which of the following is the living thing?

(a) 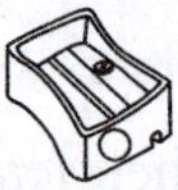 (b)  (c)  (d) 

3. Cow eats grass as cow is a ............ .

(a) living thing (b) non-living thing (c) bird (d) toy

4. Which among the following will grow in size?

(a)  (b)  (c) 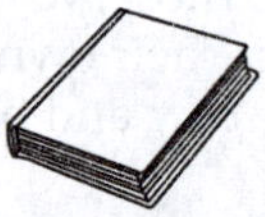 (d) 

5. Living things produce babies. Which picture shows that?

(a)  (b)  (c)  (d) 

6. Find the odd one out.

(a)  (b) 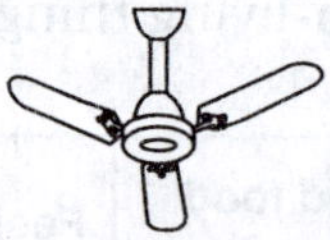 (c)  (d) 

7. Which among the following will move on its own?

(a)  (b)  (c)  (d) 

**8.** In the given pictures, identify the living things.

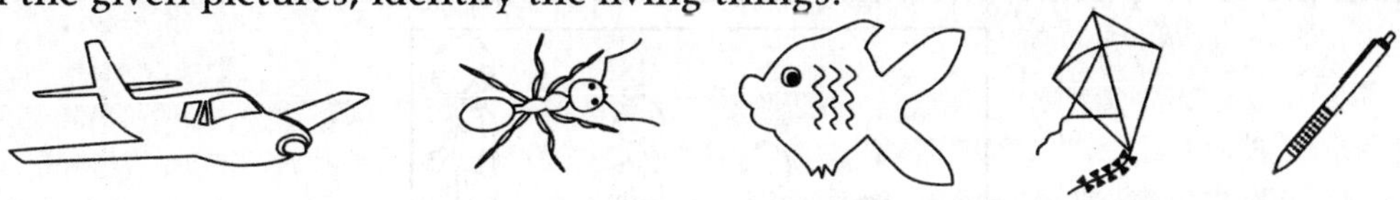

(a) Aeroplane and kite
(b) Fish and ant
(c) Pen and fish
(d) Aeroplane and pen

**9.** Which of the following is correct?
(a) Living things cannot move
(b) Non-living things can move on their own
(c) Living things can grow
(d) Non-living things need food to live

**10.** A  can run, but a .............. cannot.

(a) 
(b) 
(c) 
(d) 

**11.** .............. is a non-living thing, but .............. is a living thing.
(a) Bird, goat
(b) Dog, aeroplane
(c) Book, bird
(d) Bird, lamp

**12.** In the given picture, identify the thing that has life.

(a) Tree
(b) Road
(c) Jeep
(d) Car

**13.** Living things need .............. to live.
(a) paper
(b) sky
(c) air
(d) fan

**14.** Which action shows that living things breathe?

(a) 
(b) 
(c) 

(d) 

**15.** From the given picture, what do you know about living things?

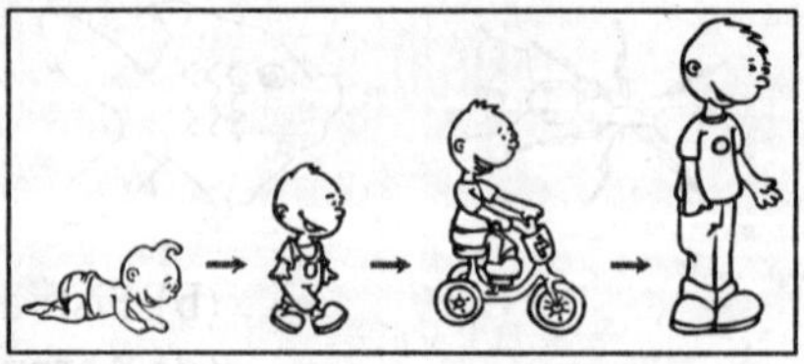

(a) Living things can move
(b) Living things can breathe
(c) Living things can reproduce
(d) Living things can grow

**16.** Select the odd one out.

(a) 
(b) 
(c) 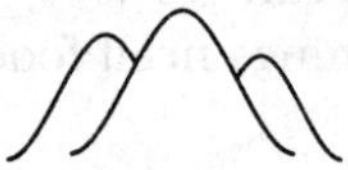
(d) 

**17.** Which word in these columns is under the wrong heading?

| Living things | Non-living things |
|---|---|
| Rose plant | Hindi book |
| Peacock | Mango tree |
| Elephant | Blue pen |

(a) Elephant
(b) Rose plant
(c) Mango tree
(d) Hindi book

**18.** All living things need air, ............... and food to live.

(a) water
(b) grass
(c) apple
(d) land

**19.** Which of the following lives in water?

(a) 
(b) 
(c) 
(d) 

**20.** Match the Column I with Column II.

| | Column I | | Column II |
|---|---|---|---|
| A. | Peacock | 1. | Can move on their own |
| B. | Box | 2. | Living thing |
| C. | Living things | 3. | Non-living thing |

**Codes**

| | A | B | C |
|---|---|---|---|
| (a) | 1 | 2 | 3 |
| (b) | 2 | 3 | 1 |
| (c) | 3 | 1 | 2 |
| (d) | 1 | 3 | 2 |

21. Which of these natural thing is living?

(a)  (b)  (c)  (d) 

22. Which one of the following is an incorrect statement?

(a) Plant is a living thing
(b) Bear is a non-living thing
(c) Cow is a living thing
(d) Table is a non-living thing

23. Which of the following living things cannot move from one place to another place?

(a)  (b)  (c)  (d) 

24. Identify the living things and choose the correct option.

(a) Shoes, Cow, Moon, Man
(b) Cow, Frog, Man, Bird
(c) Phone, Bird, House, Cow
(d) Moon, Drum, Man, Frog

25. Given picture shows a boy and a cycle. Which of the statement is not true?

(a) Both boy and cycle can move
(b) Boy can move on its own
(c) Cycle can move on its own
(d) Boy has life while cycle is lifeless

26. Which of the following things cannot live without food?

(a) A bulb
(b) A plant
(c) An aeroplane
(d) A pencil box

Chapter 02

# Plants

We see many plants around us. Plants need air, water and sunlight to make food and to grow. Various parts of plants are shown in the figure given below :

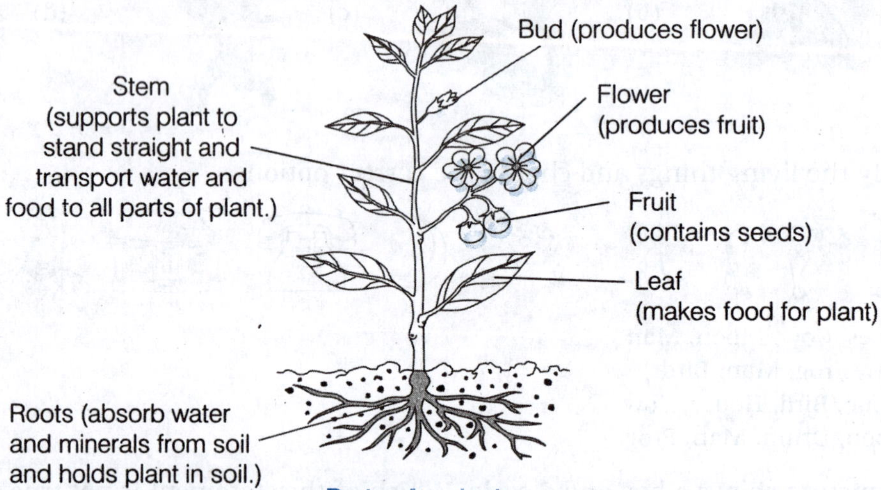

Parts of a plant

## Different Kinds of Plants

Plants may be big, small, grow on land, grow in water, etc.

- **Big plants** Plants which are big in size and have strong, woody trunk is called trees, e.g. Banyan tree, peepal tree, mango tree, etc.
- **Small plants** These are of four types
  - (i) **Shrubs** These are small plants with strong and woody stem, e.g. Rose plant, *Hibiscus* plant, jasmine plant, etc.
  - (ii) **Herbs** These are small plants with weak and green stem, e.g. Grass, spinach, mint, coriander, etc.
  - (iii) **Creepers** These plants cannot stand straight. These plants grow along the ground, e.g. Watermelon, pumpkin, etc.
  - (iv) **Climbers** These plants need support to stand straight. These have very weak stem. e.g. Grapevine, money plant, pea plant, etc.

# Let's Practice

1. The part of a plant at point *A* is .............. .

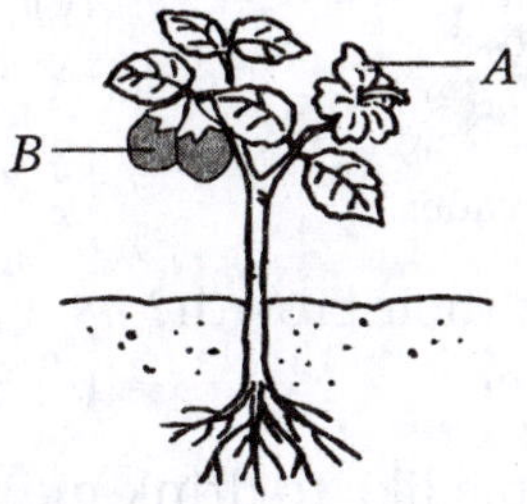


(a) grass (b) fruit (c) leaf (d) flower

2. .............. is formed in point *B*.

(a) fruit (b) root (c) stem (d) leaf

3. Very big plants with wooden stems are called .............. .

(a) climbers (b) creepers (c) trees (d) shrubs

4. Pick the odd one out.

(a)  (b)  (c)  (d) 

5. Given figure shows seed of which fruit?

(a) Papaya (b) Lemon (c) Plum (d) Mango

6. Pick the odd one out.

(a) 
Sunflower

(b) 
Radish

(c) 
Jasmine

(d) 
Rose

7. Which of the following is not a food grain?

(a)  Rice

(b)  Sugarcane

(c)  Wheat

(d)  Maize

8. What do the plants require for their growth?

(a) Air (b) Water (c) Sunlight (d) All of these

9. I comes from a shrub and people like to drink me. Who am I?

(a)  Tea

(b) 

Ghee

(c)  Milk

(d) 

Coke

**Directions** (Q. Nos. 10-12) See the picture given below and answer the questions.

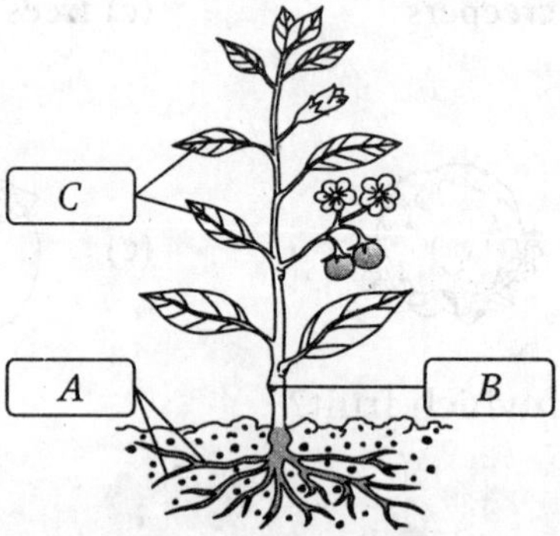


10. I hold the plant. I am present under the ground.

(a) Fruit (b) Flower (c) Root (d) Stem

11. I support the plant. Leaves, fruits, flowers grows on me.

(a) Stem (b) Root (c) Seed (d) Bud

12. I am the kitchen of the plant as I make food for it.

(a) Root (b) Fruit (c) Stem (d) Leaves

13. Which of the following fruit is form a creeper?

(a)  Apple

(b)  Orange

(c)  Watermelon

(d)  Banana

14. These are seeds 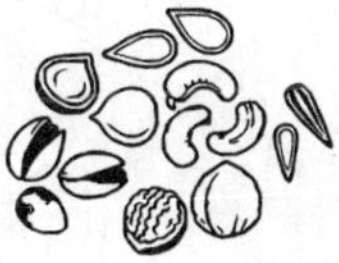 . From where do we get them?

(a) Flowers (b) Fruits (c) Roots (d) Leaves

15. ............ has just one seed in it but ........... has many seeds in it.

(a) Mango, banana
(b) Orange, guava
(c) Papaya, mango
(d) Mango, papaya

16. Which is not a part of plant?

(a) Flowers (b) Fruits (c) Roots (d) Soil

17. Which part of the plant is of different colours?

(a) Stem
(b) Leaves
(c) Flower
(d) Root

18. Which of the following statement is false?

(a) Cherry is a fruit
(b) Potato is a vegetable
(c) Rice is a grain
(d) Groundnut is a spice

19. Which of these is incorrectly matched?

| | Plants | Things we get |
|---|---|---|
| (a) |  | Sugar |
| (b) |  | Pulses |
| (c) | 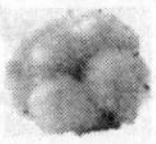 | Cotton shirt |
| (d) |  | Chapati |

20. Which of the following fruits give us oil?

(a) 

Apple

(b) 

Mango

(c) 

Coconut

(d) 

Cherry

**21.** Given fruit is grown on which plant?

(a) 

(b) 

(c) 

(d) 

**22.** Which of the following thing we do not get from plants?

(a) Fruits
(b) Clothes
(c) Medicines
(d) Plastic

**23.** Which of these contain seeds which we can eat?

(a) 

Carrot

(b) 

Apple

(c) 

Beans

(d) 

Mango

**24.** The leaf of a plant is given below with its fruit.

Which fruit is belong to such plant?

(a) 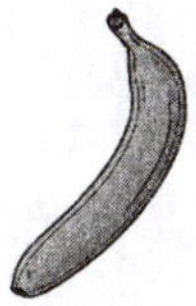 (b)  (c)  (d) 

**25.** Which of the following flowers floats on water?

(a)  (b)  (c)  (d) 

**26.** Find the correct number of fruits, flowers and vegetables from the box.

| Pumpkin | Apple | Lotus |
|---|---|---|
| Potato | Guava | |
| Brinjal | Ladyfinger | |
| Orange | Cucumber | |

(a) 2 fruits, 3 vegetables, 2 flowers
(b) 6 vegetables, 3 fruits, 2 flowers
(c) 5 vegetables, 3 fruits, 1 flower
(d) 3 vegetables, 3 fruits, 3 flowers

Chapter
03

# Animals

## Land and Water Animals

- Animals which live on land are called as **land animals**, e.g. Lion, cat, dog, cow, etc.
- Animals which live in water are called as **water animals**, e.g. Fish, dolphin, whale, octopus, etc.

## Domestic and Wild Animals

- Animals which live with us in our homes or farms are called as **domestic animals**. They are also called as **pet animals**, e.g. Dog, cat, cow, goat, etc.
- Animals which live in forests are called as **wild animals**, e.g. Lion, tiger, elephant, bear, etc.

## Birds and Insects

- Animals which have feathers and one beak are called as **birds**. Most birds can fly, e.g. Pigeon, sparrow, eagle, etc.
- Some birds have feathers, but cannot fly, e.g. Ostrich, penguin, etc.
- Some birds can swim also, e.g. Duck and swan.
- Animals which are very small in size, has six legs and have wings or no wings are called as insects, e.g. Earthworm, cockroach, butterfly, etc.

## Food of Animals

- Some animals eat plants only, e.g. Cow, elephant, horse, rabbit, etc.
- Some animals eat flesh of other animals, e.g. Lion, tiger, snake, cat, etc.
- Some animals eat both plants and flesh of other animals, e.g. Bear, dog, crow, etc.

## Homes of Animals

| | | | | | |
|---|---|---|---|---|---|
| Bear – | Den | Horse – | Stable | Rabbit – | Burrow |
| Spider – | Web | Sheep – | Fold | Dog – | Kennel |

# Let's Practice

**1.** Where do wild animals live?

(a) Homes
(b) Farms
(c) Forests
(d) Villages

**2.** Which of the following is not a wild animal?

(a) 
Tiger

(b) 
Zebra

(c) 
Cheetah

(d) 
Sheep

**3.** Which of the following is not a pet/domestic animal?

(a) 
Lion

(b) 
Buffalo

(c) 
Goat

(d) 
Dog

**4.** Which is the largest animal in the world?

(a) 
Crocodile

(b) 
Elephant

(c) 
Polar Bear

(d) 
Whale

**5.** Which of the following is not a water animal?

(a) 
Crocodile

(b) 
Fish

(c) 
Rat

(d) 
Tortoise

**6.** Which of the following is not an insect?

(a) 
Butterfly

(b) 
Ant

(c) 
Lizard

(d) 
Grasshopper

**7.** Which animal can walk easily on sand?

(a) 
Camel

(b) 
Horse

(c) 
Donkey

(d) 
Bear

**8.** Which of the following does not build a nest?

(a) 
Sparrow

(b) 
Crow

(c) 
Squirrel

(d) 
Koel

**9.** Which animal lives on trees?
(a) Monkey (b) Donkey (c) Elephant (d) Fish

**10.** What does cow like to eat?

(a) 
Eggs

(b) 
Fish

(c) 

Milk

(d) 
Grass

**11.** Animals like lion and tiger always eat .............. .
(a) milk (b) flesh (c) chapati (d) honey

**12.** Which animal can be seen in the farms?

(a) 
Stag

(b) 
Ox

(c) 
Monkey

(d) 
Fox

**13.** Which of the following cannot fly?

(a)  (b)  (c)  (d) 

**14.** There are some birds that cannot fly. Which of these birds cannot fly?

|  |  |  |  |  |  |
|---|---|---|---|---|---|
| Pigeon (1) | Owl (2) | Ostrich (3) | Kiwi (4) | Parrot (5) | Penguin (6) |

(a) 2, 3 and 4
(b) 1, 2 and 6
(c) 4, 5 and 6
(d) 3, 4 and 6

**15.** Match the animals given in Column I with their respective homes given in Column II.

| | Column I | | | Column II | |
|---|---|---|---|---|---|
| A. |  | Bird | 1. |  | Stable |
| B. |  | Honeybee | 2. |  | Nest |
| C. |  | Horse | 3. | 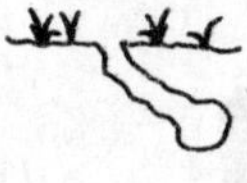 | Hole |
| D. |  | Mouse | 4. | 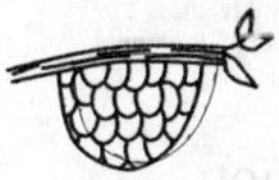 | Beehive |

**Codes**

| | A | B | C | D | | A | B | C | D |
|---|---|---|---|---|---|---|---|---|---|
| (a) | 4 | 1 | 3 | 2 | (b) | 3 | 2 | 4 | 1 |
| (c) | 2 | 4 | 1 | 3 | (d) | 3 | 1 | 2 | 4 |

16. Arrange the following letters to find the name of an animal who lives in stable?

RSHEO

(a) HEN (b) PIGEON
(c) HORSE (d) PEACOCK

17. Which of these animals kill other animals for their food?

(a) 
Lion

(b) 
Buffalo

(c) 
Horse

(d) 
Goat

18. Insects have .............. legs and birds have .............. legs.
(a) 2, 4 (b) 6, 2
(c) 4, 2 (d) 4, 4

19. Which of the following is not correctly match?
(a) Birds — Grain
(b) Lion—Flesh
(c) Deer—Both plants and flesh
(d) Cow—Grass

20. Select the option that correctly arrange the given animals in increasing order of their size (smallest to biggest).

(A) 
(B) 
(C) 

Choose the correct option.
(a) C < B < A (b) A < B < C
(c) B < C < A (d) A < C < B

**Directions** (Q.Nos. 21-23) Arun saw many animals in the zoo. But he forget their names when telling about them to his mother. Help him to identify those animals.

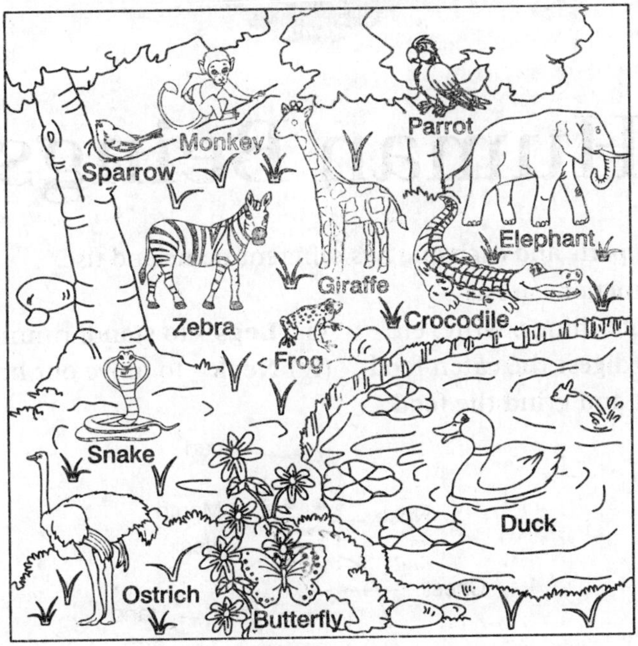


Answers the questions with the help of given figure above.

21. This animal has no hands or legs and only crawls.
(a) Crocodile (b) Snake (c) Monkey (d) Frog

22. This bird lays egg like hen but swims easily in water.
(a) Duck (b) Sparrow (c) Ostrich (d) Parrot

23. This animal has a tall neck and brown spots on its body.
(a) Elephant (b) Parrot (c) Zebra (d) Giraffe

24. Which of the following animal lays egg?

(a) 
Hen

(b) 
Cow

(c) 
Buffalo

(d) 
Lion

25. Which of the following is not true?
(a) Dog guards our home (b) Deer gives us milk
(c) Sheep gives us wool (d) Donkey carries load

# Chapter 04

# Human Beings

- Our body has many parts and each one has different name and use.
- Some body parts functions are as
  (i) **Hands** - to hold things, write, etc.
  (ii) **Legs** - to stand, running, walking, etc.
  (iii) **Stomach** - to digest the eaten food.
  (iv) **Neck** - to move our head.
  (v) **Teeth** - to cut and grind the food.

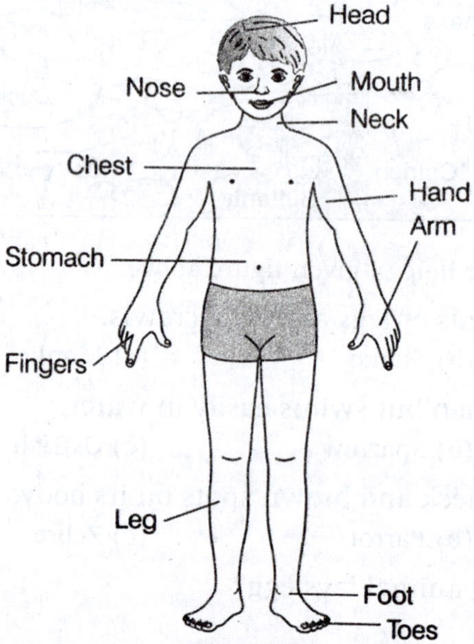


**Body parts**

## Sense Organs

Sense organs helps us to know the world around us, we have five sense organs as follows

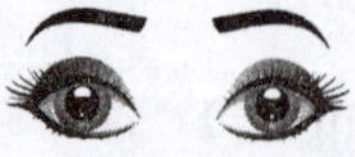

**Eyes**
Helps us to see

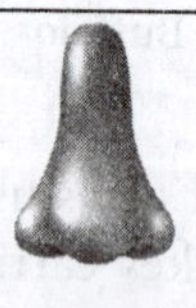

**Nose**
Helps us to smell

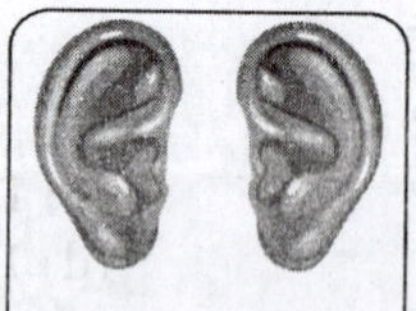

**Ears**
Helps us to hear

**Tongue**
Helps us to taste

**Skin**
Helps us to feel

# Let's Practice

1. The human body has ........... sense organs.

(a) six (b) seven (c) two (d) five

2. When you see a cartoon, which sense organ do you use?

(a) 
Ear

(b) 
Nose

(c) 
Eye

(d) 
Tongue

3. Your mother is making tasty food. You smell it with ............... .

(a) 
Eye

(b) 
Skin

(c) 
Ear

(d) 
Nose

4. When we hold a hot cup of tea, we instantly remove our hands. Which sense organ tells us that the tea is hot?

(a) Eye (b) Skin (c) Ears (d) Nose

5. While listening to music, we are using our ............... .

(a) 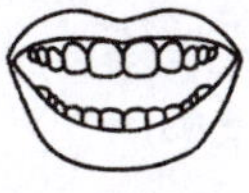
Teeth

(b) 
Ear

(c) 
Eye

(d) 
Hands

6. Which part of the body is used to cut and chew the food?

(a) 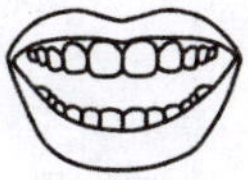
Teeth

(b) 
Nose

(c) 
Eye

(d) 
Ear

7. Pick the odd one out.

(a) 
Knee

(b) 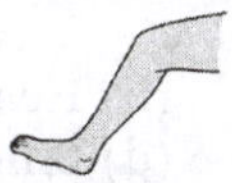
Leg

(c) 
Eye

(d) 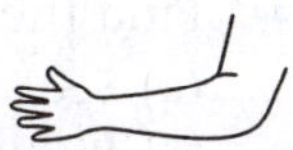
Elbow

8. You drank a bitter coffee. Which of the following organ is used?
(a) Teeth (b) Tongue (c) Nose (d) Ear

9. Nails are part of our......
(a) fingers (b) knee (c) chest (d) ears

10. You are sweating in summer. By which of the following organ you sense heat?
(a) Nose (b) Eyes (c) Ears (d) Skin

11. We play carrom with the help of our ............ .
(a) ears and hands (b) hands and legs (c) hands and eyes (d) nose and legs

12. Match the sense organs given in Column I with their functions given in Column II.

| | Column I | | | Column II | |
|---|---|---|---|---|---|
| A. |  | Eye | 1. |  | Smell |
| B. |  | Nose | 2. |  | Taste |
| C. |  | Ear | 3. |  | Read |
| D. |  | Tongue | 4. |  | Hear |

**Codes**

| | A | B | C | D | | A | B | C | D |
|---|---|---|---|---|---|---|---|---|---|
| (a) | 3 | 1 | 4 | 2 | (b) | 4 | 2 | 3 | 1 |
| (c) | 2 | 3 | 4 | 1 | (d) | 1 | 4 | 3 | 2 |

13. Which of the following body parts are two in number?
(a) Head (b) Chest
(c) Ears (d) Nose

14. You going to school carry your school bags on your......
(a) legs (b) shoulder
(c) chest (d) head

15. Find the odd one out.
(a) See (b) Hear
(c) Jump (d) Smell

16. Which is not a part of sense organ?
(a) Skin (b) Nose
(c) Hairs (d) Ears

**17.** When we eat food where does it goes?
(a) into the stomach (b) into the lungs (c) into the kidney (d) into the brain

**18.** Which of the following pairs is incorrectly matched?
(a) Hand - write (b) Skin - smell
(c) Leg - walk (d) Eyes - sight

**19.** Fingers are there in our hands.
(a) 10 (b) 20
(c) 5 (d) 15

**20.** Which of the following pairs is incorrect?
(a) Eye - television (b) Ear - perfume
(c) Tongue - pizza (d) Nose - flowers

**21.** The figure given represents the sense of ............... .

(a) smell (b) taste
(c) hearing (d) touch

**22.** The item given below is used for

(a)  (b) 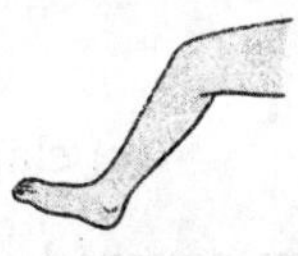 (c) 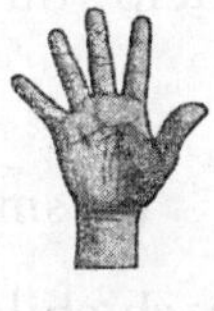 (d) 

**23.** Which of the following activities can be done by using legs?

(a) 
Walking

(b) 
Eating

(c) 
Reading

(d) 
Combing

**24.** Label the parts *P, Q, R* and *S* respectively.

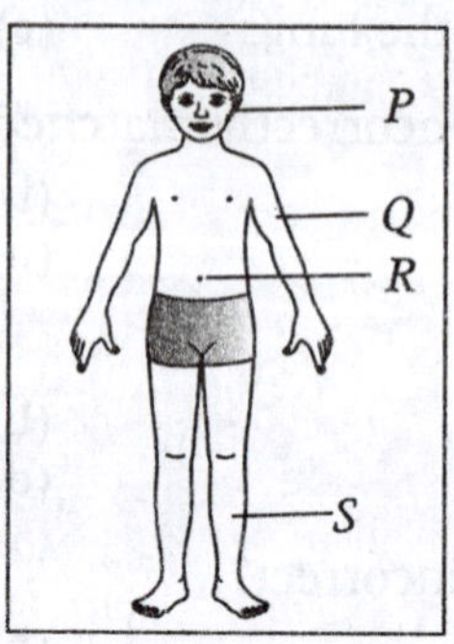


(a) Eye, Nose, Brain, Leg
(b) Nose, Leg, Head, Stomach
(c) Ear, Hand, Stomach, Leg
(d) Eye, Nose, Ear, Head

**25.** Fill in the blanks to complete the poem.

Two little ........... to look around.
Two little ears to hear each sound.
One little ........... to smell what's sweets.
One little mouth that likes to eat.

(a) eyes, hand (b) eyes, nose (c) hands, nose (d) hands, leg

**26.** What can we taste?

(a) 
Food substances

(b) 

Television

(c) 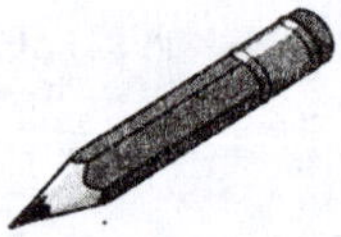
Pencil

(d) 
Kite

**27.** 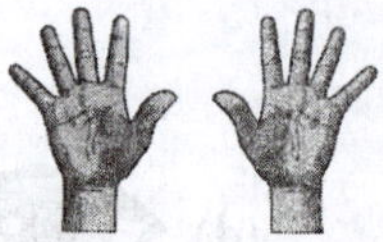 will help you to

(a) sing a song (b) smell perfumes (c) clap for cheers (d) see pictures

**28.** One sense organ of each children has been covered

Raj

Kush

Shalu

Which children cannot see the rainbow after raining?

(a) Raj
(b) Kush
(c) Raj and Shalu
(d) Kush and Shalu

Chapter
05

# Safety Rules and First Aid

## At Home

Do not play with sharp objects.

Do not touch electric plugs and switches with wet hands.

Do not play with fire.

## At School

Do not stand on the desk or chairs.

Always stand in a queue while get in the bus.

Do not take out any body part out of the moving bus.

Do not run fastly on the stairs.

## In Playground

- Always play in the playground.
- Always follow the rules of the game.
- Do not fight with others while playing.

## First Aid

First aid is the first medical help given to the injured or sick person, before the doctor arrives.

First aid box contains-Scissors, band-aid, antiseptic lotion, cotton roll, etc.

## On Road

Always walk on footpath.

Do not play on the road.

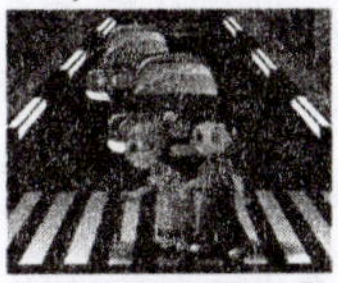
Always use zebra crossing to cross the road.

# Let's Practice

**1.** Which is not a colour of traffic light?

(a) Red (b) Black (c) Green (d) Yellow

**2.** Which of the following is not a good habit?

(a) 
Washing hands before eating

(b) 
Brushing teeth twice a day

(c) 
Doing exercises regularly

(d) 
Getting up late in the morning

**3.** Which of the following thing can hurt you?

(a) 
Comb

(b) 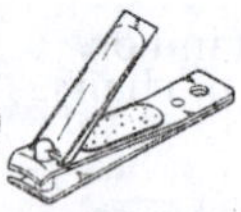
Nail cutter

(c) 
Toothbrush

(d) 

Soap

**4.** It is a bad habit to ……

(a) 
Bath everyday

(b) 
Wash hands after toilet

(c) 
Throw things in a dustbin

(d) 
Plucking flowers and leaves

**5.** ……… should not be touched with wet hands.

(a) 
Electric Switch

(b) 
Toys

(c) 
Comb

(d) 
Flowers

**6.** You should not play with

(a) friends (b) pets

(c) sharp tools (d) parents

**7.** Match the following columns.

| | Column I | | Column II |
|---|---|---|---|
| A. | Red light | 1. | Stop |
| B. | Green light | 2. | Ready to move |
| C. | Yellow light | 3. | Move |

**Codes**

| | A | B | C | | A | B | C |
|---|---|---|---|---|---|---|---|
| (a) | 1 | 2 | 3 | (b) | 2 | 1 | 3 |
| (c) | 1 | 3 | 2 | (d) | 3 | 2 | 1 |

**8.** What will you say when you pushed someone by mistake?

(a) Sorry
(b) Thank you
(c) Welcome
(d) None of these

**9.** Select the correct match of the activity and the place where it should be practised.

| | Activity | | Place |
|---|---|---|---|
| (a) | Playing football | - | On Road |
| (b) | Standing | - | On Desk |
| (c) | Walking slowly | - | On Stairs |
| (d) | Bathing | - | In Kitchen |

**10.** While going out to play in the playground, which safety rule should be followed?

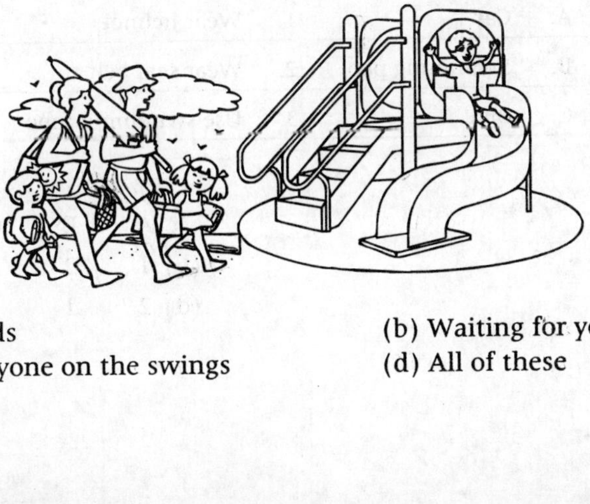

(a) Play with friends
(b) Waiting for your turn
(c) Do not push anyone on the swings
(d) All of these

**11.** Identify the things that you put in a first aid box?

1 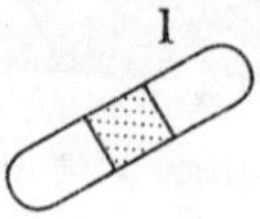 Band-Aid

2  Dettol

3 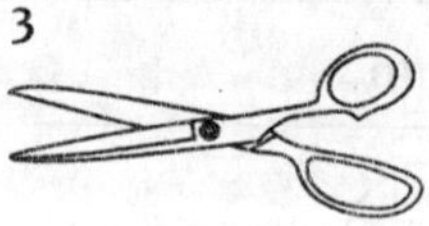 Scissors

4 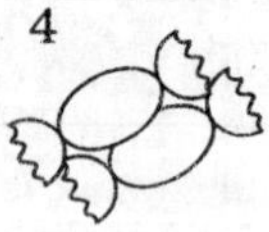 Toffees

5 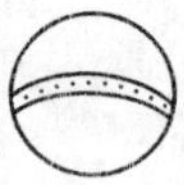 Ball

(a) 2 and 3  (b) 1, 2 and 3  (c) 3, 4 and 5  (d) 4 and 5

**12.** Which of the following figures shows zebra crossing?

(a)   (b)   (c)   (d) 

**13.** Which of the following is the safety rules, while travelling in a bus?

(a) Getting into the bus in a line

(b) Putting hands out of the vehicle

(c) Moving out of running bus

(d) Disturbing the driver, while driving

**14.** Match the following columns.

| | Column I | | Column II |
|---|---|---|---|
| A. | Car | 1. | Wear helmet |
| B. | Swimming pool | 2. | Wear seat belt |
| C. | Bike | 3. | Use swimming tube |

**Codes**

| | A | B | C |
|---|---|---|---|
| (a) | 2 | 3 | 1 |
| (b) | 1 | 2 | 3 |
| (c) | 3 | 2 | 1 |
| (d) | 2 | 1 | 3 |

**15.** Which of these things are not safe to use by small children?

1. 2. 3. 4. 5. 6.

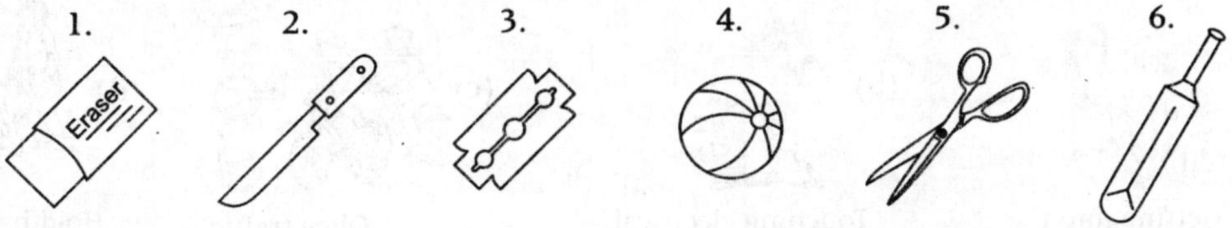


(a) 1, 5 and 6 (b) 2, 3 and 5
(c) 2, 4 and 6 (d) 1, 4 and 6

**16.** Where should we walk on the road?
(a) Zebra Crossing (b) Middle of the road
(c) Footpath (d) None of these

**17.** We should always cross the road from .............. .
(a) never cross the road (b) zebra crossing
(c) footpath (d) All of these

**18.** The three lights of the traffic signal is red, yellow and green. What does the red light indicate?
(a) Wait (b) Go
(c) Stop (d) Play

**19.** The person standing at the side of the road is .............. .
(a) traffic police (b) teacher
(c) sweeper (d) army man

**20.** Draw  if statement is correct and  if it is incorrect.

I. Do not run on the stairs II. Never play with fire
III. Jump from a moving bus

**Codes**

I II III

(a) 

I II III

(b) 

(c) 

(d) 

**21.** Children should never go into the swimming pool ........... .
(a) alone (b) with their parents
(c) with their coach (d) with their teacher

**22.** Which of the following activity should not be done by the children?

(a) 

Getting into the bus in a line

(b) 

Touching electrical switches

(c) 

Obey traffic rules

(d) 

Hold hands while crossing the road

**23.** Which of the following is a correct safety rule ?

(a) 

Placing hand outside the bus window

(b) 

Disturbing the driver

(c) 

Playing with sharp things

(d) 

Going when the green light appears

**24.** When someone gets injured, we use ............... .

(a) third aid
(b) second aid
(c) first aid
(d) fourth aid

**25.** We should cross the road when the traffic light is .............. .

(a) red
(b) green
(c) yellow
(d) orange

**26.** Which of the following signs indicate 'No Parking zone'?

(a) 

(b) 

(c) 

(d) 

Chapter 06

# Air, Water and Weather

## Air

- Air is present everywhere, we cannot see it, but we can feel it.
- Moving air is called **wind**.
- All living things need air to breathe.
- Slow moving wind is called **breeze**.
- Very fast moving wind that mostly comes with rain, thunder and lightning is called **storm**.

- Air has weight, fill space and it is colourless and tasteless.

## Water

- We get water from rain. Rainwater fills rivers, lakes, ponds and oceans.
- We need water for many things to do like washing, bathing, etc.

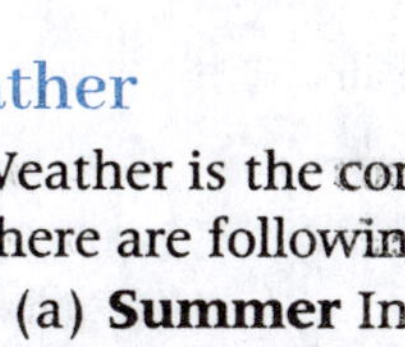

For cooking food

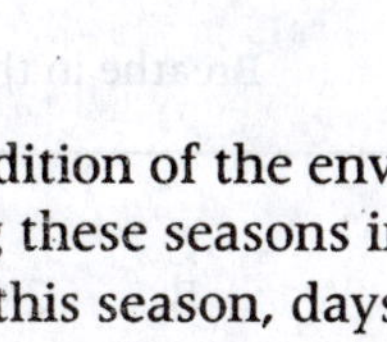

Washing utensils

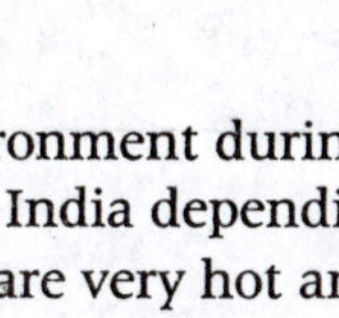

For drinking

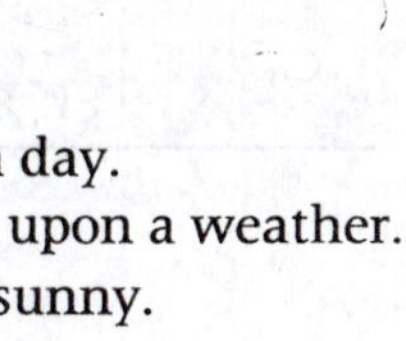

For washing clothes



Putting out fire

## Weather

- Weather is the condition of the environment during a day.
- There are following these seasons in India depending upon a weather.
  - (a) **Summer** In this season, days are very hot and sunny.
  - (b) **Autumn** In this season, trees shed their leaves.
  - (c) **Winter** In this season, days are very cold.

# Let's Practice

**1.** Which of the following cannot be seen, but is present everywhere in the nature?

(a) Sun (b) Air (c) Sky (d) Water

**2.** Which of the following do not need air to breathe?

(a)  (b)  (c)  (d) 

**3.** Which of the following is not true?

(a) Air has weight (b) Air fills space (c) Air is red in colour (d) Air can be feel

**4.** Moving air is called ............ .

(a) water (b) wind (c) storm (d) smoke

**5.** Match the following columns.

| Column I | | Column II |
|---|---|---|
| A.  | 1. | Fly in the air |
| B.  | 2. | Dry in the air |
| C.  | 3. | Breathe in the air |

**Codes**

| | A | B | C | | A | B | C |
|---|---|---|---|---|---|---|---|
| (a) | 3 | 1 | 2 | (b) | 1 | 3 | 2 |
| (c) | 1 | 2 | 3 | (d) | 3 | 2 | 1 |

**6.** Which picture shows that the day is rainy?

(a)  (b)  (c)  (d) 

**7.** In which activity, water is not needed?

(a) 
Watering the plants

(b) 
Bathing

(c) 
Cleaning the floor

(d) 
Sleeping

**8.** Rainwater fills

(a) river (b) lake (c) pond (d) All of these

**9.** 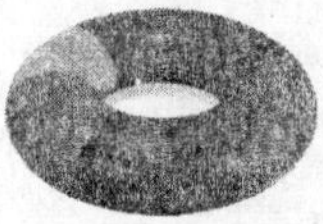 and 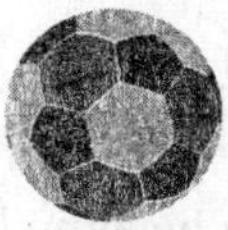 are filled with which of the following?

(a) Paper (b) Air (c) Sand (d) Clothes

**10.** Which of the following can store maximum quantity of water?

(a)  (b)  (c)  (d) All of these

**11.** What is the colour of water?

(a) Red (b) Yellow (c) Green (d) Colourless

**12.** In which season days are very cold?

(a) Summer (b) Rainy (c) Winter (d) All of these

**13.** Suppose you are thirsty. Which of the following you would avoid to get drinking water?

(a) River (b) Groundwater (d) Swamp (d) Waterfall

**14.** In which of the following activities the air gets dirty?

(a)  (b)  (c)  (d) 

**15.** Refer to the picture given below

It shows a .........

(a) hot day (b) rainy day (c) cold day (d) cloudy day

**16.** What happens if you drink dirty water?

(a) You become fit (b) You become healthy

(c) You become sick (d) You become strong

**17.** Match the following columns.

| | Column I | | Column II |
|---|---|---|---|
| A. |  | 1. | Rainy |
| B. |  | 2. | Sunny |
| C. |  | 3. | Windy |
| D. |  | 4. | Cloudy |

**Codes**

| | A | B | C | D | | A | B | C | D |
|---|---|---|---|---|---|---|---|---|---|
| (a) | 1 | 3 | 4 | 2 | (b) | 3 | 1 | 2 | 4 |
| (c) | 2 | 4 | 1 | 3 | (d) | 4 | 3 | 2 | 1 |

**Directions** (Q.Nos. 18-19) Look at the following weather chart and answer the following questions.

| Day | Monday | Tuesday | Wednesday | Thursday |
|---|---|---|---|---|
| Morning |  |  |  |  |

**18.** According to the weather report, which day is windy?

(a) Monday (b) Thursday
(c) Tuesday (d) Wednesday

**19.** According to the weather report, which is the hottest day?

(a) Thursday (b) Monday
(c) Wednesday (d) Tuesday

**20.** Which activity making water polluted/dirty?

(a)  (b)  (c)  (d) 

Chapter 07

# Our Universe

- In our universe, we have the Sun, the Moon, stars, planets, etc.
- There are eight planets in this universe which moves around the Sun.
- We live on planet Earth.

## The Sun

- The Sun gives us heat and light.
- The Sun looks like a big ball of fire.
- The Sun rises in the East and sets in the West.

Sun

## The Moon

- The Moon moves around the Earth.
- The Moon changes its shape every night.
- The Moon does not have its own light. It only reflects Sun's light.

Moon

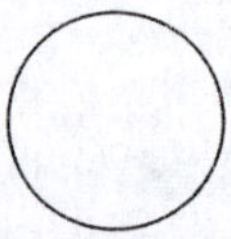

Full Moon

Half Moon

Crescent Moon

## Stars

- There are so many stars present in the sky.
- The Sun is also a star.
- Stars twinkle at night.

# Let's Practice

**1.** Which of the following things can be seen in the sky?

(a)  Sun

(b)  Star

(c)  Moon

(d) All of these

**2.** What is the shape of the Sun?

(a) 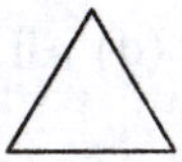

(b) 

(c) 

(d) 

**3.** Which of the following statement about Sun is not true?

(a) Sun gives us heat
(b) Sun is a planet
(c) Sun gives us light
(d) Sun shines during the day

**4.** Rising, rising the Sun is rising. Going, going darkness is going.
The Sun rises from which direction?

(a) West (b) South (c) East (d) North

**5.** Very big and bright ball of fire in the sky is known as ........... .

(a) Sun (b) Moon (c) North Star (d) None of these

**6.** The Sun sets in the ...............

(a) East (b) North (c) South (d) West

**7.** Identify the things that can be seen in the night sky.

(a) Sun (b) Moon (c) Stars (d) Both (b) and (c)

8. Every night it can be seen in a different shape. What is it?
(a) River (b) Moon
(c) Mountain (d) Sky

9. How many planets are present in the solar system?
(a) Eight (b) Six
(c) Seven (d) Five

10. Which of the following is a star?

(a) 
The Sun

(b) 
The Moon

(c) 
The Earth

(d) All of these

11. Which of the following shape is never taken by the Moon?

(a) 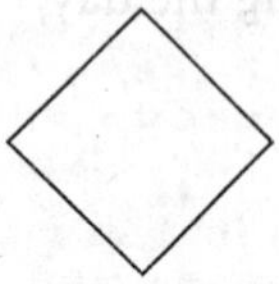 (b)  (c)  (d) 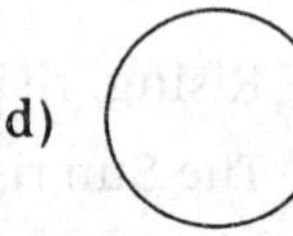

12. This is a vehicle that can take you to the Moon. What is it called?

(a) Helicopter (b) Parachute
(c) Rocket (d) Aeroplane

13. Can you count the number of stars in the night sky?
(a) Yes, I can count (b) Yes, it is 100
(c) May be more than 100 (d) No, it is not possible

14. Identify the shape in which the stars appear to us.

(a) 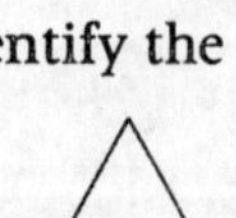 (b) 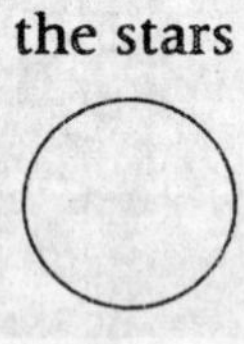 (c)  (d) 

**15.** Where do all plants, land and water animals and humans live?

(a) 
Sun

(b) 
Earth

(c) 
Star

(d) 
Moon

**16.** Which of the following is closest star to the Earth?

(a) Moon
(b) Sun
(c) Mars
(d) None of these

**17.** Moon can be seen ............... .

(a) at night
(b) in morning
(c) all day
(d) at evening

**18.** Which of the following is a planet?

(a) 
Sun

(b) 
Earth

(c) 
Star

(d) 
Moon

**19.** Moon moves around the ............... .

(a) Earth
(b) Sun
(c) Stars
(d) Our house

# PRACTICE SET 01

**1.** Which of the following animal does not live in forest?

(a) Deer (b) Lion (c) Rabbit (d) Penguin

**2.** Which shape is not taken by the Moon?

(a) 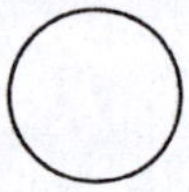
Full Moon

(b) 
Crescent Moon

(c) 
Half Moon

(d) 
Gibbous Moon

**3.**  is kept on the ...... to listen to the songs.

(a) ears (b) legs (c) hands (d) eyes

**4.** Which of the following fruits have many number of seeds in it?

(a) 

(b) 

(c) 

(d) 

**5.** Match the following columns.

| Column I | Column II |
|---|---|
| A.  | 1. Doing exercise |
| B. 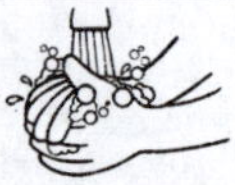 | 2. Cutting nails |
| C. 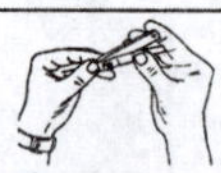 | 3. Brushing teeth |
| D.  | 4. Washing hands |

**Codes**

| | A | B | C | D |
|---|---|---|---|---|
| (a) | 1 | 4 | 3 | 2 |
| (b) | 3 | 4 | 2 | 1 |
| (c) | 2 | 1 | 4 | 3 |
| (d) | 4 | 3 | 1 | 2 |

**6.** ...... moves in search of food.

(a) An aeroplane (b) An elephant (c) A car (d) A *Cactus*

**7.** What is filled inside all of these?

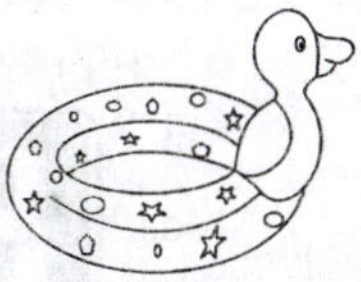

Swimming tube

Balloon

Football

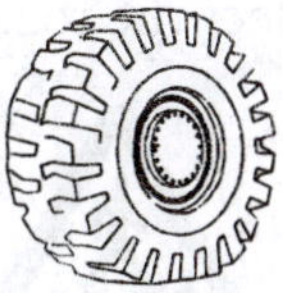

Tyre

(a) Water (b) Gun (c) Air (d) None of these

**8.** Ankit is using which sense organs to do the following activity?

(a)  Ears and Nose

(b)  Eyes, Ears and Hand

(c)  Tongue and Nose

(d)  Skin and Tongue

**9.** Select the type of plants shown below.

A.  B.  C.  D. 

| | A | B | C | D |
|---|---|---|---|---|
| (a) | Tree | Herb | Creeper | Shrub |
| (b) | Creeper | Climber | Tree | Herb |
| (c) | Herb | Shrub | Climber | Creeper |
| (d) | Creeper | Shrub | Climber | Herb |

**10.** We should keep the rivers clean because ...... .

1. all living beings drink water from it. 2. dirty water pollutes the river.

(a) Only 1 (b) Both 1 and 2 (c) Only 2 (d) None of these

**11.** Which of the following statement is true?

1. Tiger eats grass and leaves. 2. Fish lives in water. 3. Pet animals live in forest.

(a) Only 2 (b) Only 3 (c) 2 and 3 (d) 1 and 4

**12.** Select the road sign that represents men can cross the road.

(a)  (b)  (c)  (d) 

**13.** We see the Sun, the Moon and stars in the

The Sun The Moon A Star

(a) home (b) school (c) sky (d) bedroom

**14.** Ravi got a teddy bear  and a little puppy  on his birthday. On his next birthday what will happen?

(a) Teddy bear will grow (b) Both will grow
(c) Little puppy will grow (d) None of these

**15.** Fill in the blanks by choosing the correct option.

We should drink ...... water. Drinking ...... water can cause many ...... .

(a) pure, pure, diseases (b) impure, pure, diseases
(c) pure, impure, diseases (d) impure, impure, diseases

**16.** The colour of the teeth is ....... .

(a) white (b) pink (c) orange (d) green

**17.** Neem, tulsi are some plants that give us which of the following?

(a) 
Fruits

(b) 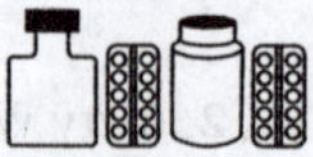
Medicine

(c) 
Rubber

(d) 
Vegetables

**18.** The shape of the Earth and others planet is like a

(a) 
Square

(b) 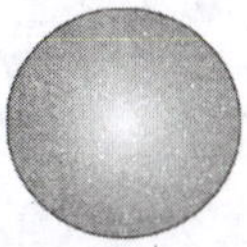
Circle

(c) 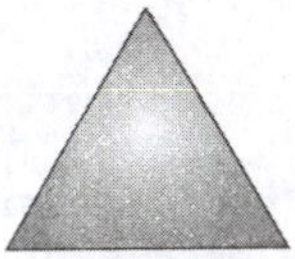
Triangle

(d) 
Rectangle

**19.** Which of the following cannot be found in a first aid box?

(a) 
Scissors

(b) 
Band-aid

(c) 

Matchstick

(d) 
Medicine

**20.** Match the following columns.

| Column I (Animals) | Column II (Food) |
|---|---|
| A.  | 1.  |
| B.  | 2.  |
| C.  | 3.  |

**Codes**

| | A | B | C | | A | B | C |
|---|---|---|---|---|---|---|---|
| (a) | 1 | 2 | 3 | (b) | 3 | 2 | 1 |
| (c) | 1 | 3 | 2 | (d) | 2 | 3 | 1 |

**21.** Which of the following pictures show both a living and a non-living things together?

(a) 

Fish in a fish bowl

(b) 

Pencil in a pencil box

(c) 

Birds living on a tree

(d) 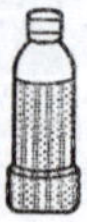

Water in a bottle

**22.** Which of the following is true about air?

(a) Air is red in colour
(b) Air is sweet in taste
(c) Sometimes air is hot and sometimes it is cold
(d) Air is not present everywhere

**23.** Choose the correct group of animal and plant products.

| | Animal Food | Plant Food |
|---|---|---|
| A. | Idli, honey, bread | Butter, fruit, juice |
| B. | Fruit, juice, butter | Idli, bread, honey |
| C. | Bread, idli | Butter, fruit, juice, honey |
| D. | Butter, honey | Idli, fruit, juice, bread |

**24.** Match the following columns.

| | Column I | | Column II |
|---|---|---|---|
| A. |  | 1. | Crossing the road |
| B. |  | 2. | Swimming |
| C. | 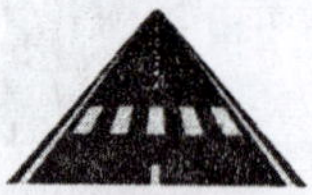 | 3. | Driving |
| D. |  | 4. | Cycling |

**Codes**

| | A | B | C | D | | A | B | C | D |
|---|---|---|---|---|---|---|---|---|---|
| (a) | 1 | 2 | 3 | 4 | (b) | 3 | 1 | 4 | 2 |
| (c) | 2 | 4 | 1 | 3 | (d) | 4 | 3 | 2 | 1 |

**25.** Which of the following things in the garden are non-living?

(a) *K* and *N* (b) *K* and *L* (c) *M* and *N* (d) *L* and *M*

**26.** Which of the following is the part of the hand?

(a) Eyes (b) Knee (c) Ear (d) Elbow

**27.** Which of the following do we see during the day?

(a) 

The Sun

(b) 

A Star

(c) 

The Moon

(d) 

The Earth

**28.** Which of the following statement is incorrect about them?

(a) All are birds
(b) All have one beak without teeth
(c) All have two legs
(d) All can fly

**29.** Which of the following cannot move from its place?

(a) 

(b) 

(c) 

(d) All of these

**30.** We get milk from

(a) 
Cow

(b) 
Buffalo

(c) 
Goat

(d) All of these

**31.** Who among the following children is/are obeying safety rules?

(a) 

(b) 

(c) 

(d) 

**32.** There are ...... stars are present in the sky.

(a) two only (b) three only (c) twenty only (d) so many

**33.** Which plant part give rise to a flower?

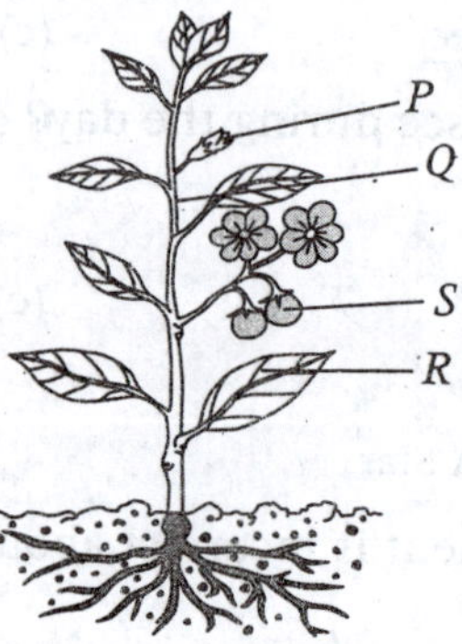


(a) *P* only (b) *Q* only (c) *R* only (d) *S* only

**34.** Which of the following is not a part of our leg?

(a) Ankle (b) Knee (c) Thighs (d) Wrist

**35.** Mark ☺ for correct statement and ☹ for incorrect statement.

I. Air and water are living things.
II. We should save water.
III. We should keep the air clean.

| | I | II | III |
|---|---|---|---|
| (a) | ☺ | ☺ | ☺ |
| (b) | ☹ | ☺ | ☹ |
| (c) | ☹ | ☺ | ☺ |
| (d) | ☺ | ☹ | ☹ |

# PRACTICE SET 02

**1.** Pick the odd one out .

(a)  (b)  (c)  (d) 

**2.** The animal shown in the picture is kept in a

(a) shed (b) kennel (c) stable (d) coop

**3.** Which of the following objects are safe to play?

(1)

(2)

(3)

(4)

(a) 1 and 2 (b) 2 and 3 (c) 3 and 4 (d) 1 and 4

**4.** Planets move around the ...... .

(a)  (b)  (c)  (d) None of these

**5.** Which of the pair is wrongly matched?

| | Column I | | Column II |
|---|---|---|---|
| (a) |  | 1. | Tree |
| (b) |  | 2. | Herb |
| (c) |  | 3. | Shrub |
| (d) |  | 4. | Climber |

**6.** How many eyes are there in our human body?

(a) 5 (b) 4 (c) 2 (d) 1

**7.** The activity shown in the figure makes water.

Boiling of water

(a) dirty (b) colourful (c) pure (d) sweet

**8.** Find the odd one out.

(a)  Bee
(b)  Mosquito
(c)  Ant
(d)  Butterfly

**9.** Which of the following you cannot count on your fingers?

(a) 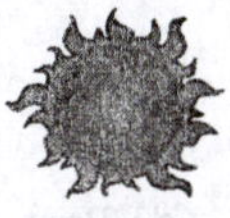
(b) 
(c) 
(d) 

**10.** Which part of the body is the boy used to hold the racket?

(a) Legs
(b) Hands
(c) Neck
(d) Stomach

**11.** Consider the following statements which is correct?

I. All living things move by itself.
II. Plants are living things.

(a) Only I is correct
(b) Only II is correct
(c) Both I and II are correct
(d) Both I and II are incorrect

**12.** See the following pictures and find out which statement is true?

*A*

*B*

*C*

(a) They all are following safety rules
(b) Boy in *C* is following safety rule
(c) Boy in *A* is following safety rule
(d) They all are not following safety rules

**13.** In the given figure, which labelled part of the plant is known as kitchen of the plant?

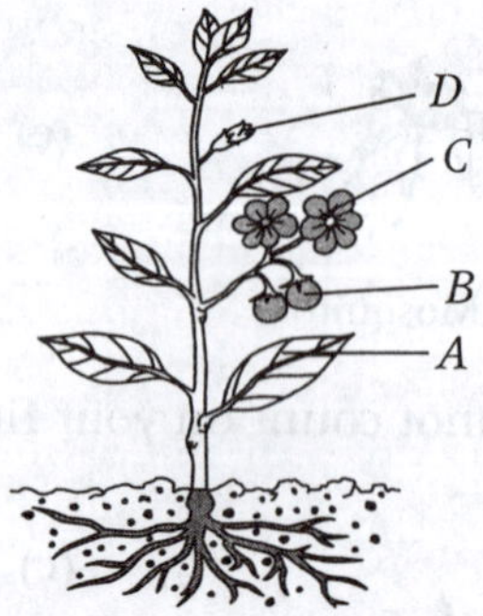


(a) Part *D* (b) Part *C* (c) Part *B* (d) Part *A*

**14.** Which of the following is needed by the boy to flying the kite?

(a) Air (b) Water (c) Food (d) Clothes

**15.** Match the sense organs given in Column I with their functions given in Column II.

| Column I | Column II |
|---|---|
| A.  Eye | 1.  Smell |
| B.  Nose | 2.  Taste |
| C.  Ear | 3.  Read |
| D.  Tongue | 4.  Hear |

**Codes**

| | A | B | C | D | | A | B | C | D |
|---|---|---|---|---|---|---|---|---|---|
| (a) | 3 | 1 | 4 | 2 | (b) | 4 | 2 | 3 | 1 |
| (c) | 2 | 3 | 4 | 1 | (d) | 1 | 4 | 3 | 2 |

**16.** Arrange the pictures in order starting from seed to tree.

A. 
B. 
C. 
D. 

(a) $B \rightarrow D \rightarrow A \rightarrow C$
(b) $D \rightarrow A \rightarrow C \rightarrow B$
(c) $A \rightarrow B \rightarrow D \rightarrow C$
(d) $C \rightarrow B \rightarrow D \rightarrow A$

**17.** The following items are used in which season?

(a) Winter
(b) Summer
(c) Rainy
(d) Autumn

**18.** The given picture shows the home of ...... .

(a) Butterfly
(b) Ant
(c) Spider
(d) Honeybee

**19.** Pick the odd one out.

(a) 
Play on the road

(b) 
Get off a moving bus

(c) 
Crossing at zebra crossing

(d) 
Placing hand outside the bus window

**20.** Moon 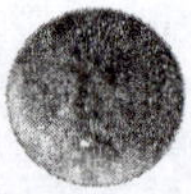 moves around the

(a) Sun (b) Earth (c) Star (d) None of these

**21.** All living things need ......, ...... and food to live.

(a) air, water (b) day, night (c) chips, chocolate (d) sea, land

**22.** These clothes are required in which season?

(a) Summer (b) Autumn (c) Winter (d) Rainy

**23.** Match the following.

| | | Product | | | Part of the plant |
|---|---|---|---|---|---|
| A. |  | Mustard Oil | 1. |  | Trunk |
| B. |  | Cotton Shirt | 2. |  | Seeds |
| C. |  | Chair | 3. |  | Cotton flower |

**Codes**

| | A | B | C | | A | B | C |
|---|---|---|---|---|---|---|---|
| (a) | 2 | 3 | 1 | (b) | 3 | 2 | 1 |
| (c) | 1 | 2 | 3 | (d) | 2 | 1 | 3 |

**24.** Raghav is reading a book. Which body parts is he using, a while doing it?

(a) Hands (b) Legs (c) Ears (d) Eyes

**25.** Raju stood in front of the window and saw the Sun rising. In which direction is his window?

(a) East (b) North (c) West (d) South

**26.** What is first aid?

(a) First treatment given to a patient
(b) Giving food to hungry people
(c) Looking after animals
(d) Helping the old people

**27.** Consider the following two statements. Which of the statement is correct?

I. Animals like cow, goat, buffalo give us milk.

II. All animals do not give us milk.

(a) Only I is correct
(b) Only II is correct
(c) Both I and II are correct
(d) Both I and II are incorrect

**28.** Which of the following thing is wrongly placed?

| **Living thing** | | **Non-living thing** | | |
|---|---|---|---|---|
|  | 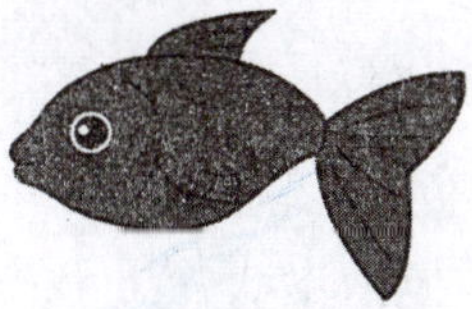 |  |  |  |
| Tree | Fish | Chair | Aeroplane | Bird |

(a) Tree (b) Bird (c) Fish (d) Chair

**29.** When we keep water in the freezer then the water forms

(a) 
Steam

(b) 
Ice

(c) 
Snow

(d) 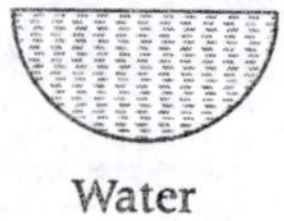
Water

**30.** What are these?

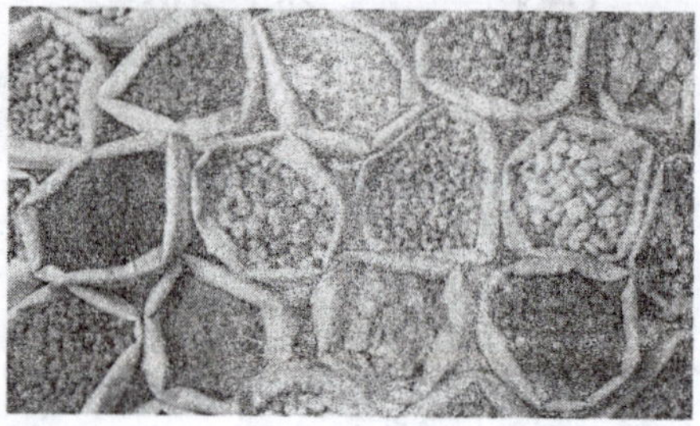

(a) Vegetables (b) Fruits (c) flowers (d) Pulses

**31.** Which of the following should not be done while crossing the road?

1. Using zebra crossing
2. Talking on the mobile
3. Running
4. Listening to music

(a) Only 1 (b) Only 2 and 3 (c) 2, 3 and 4 (d) Only 1 and 2

**32.** Which of the following things given below can grow after some days?

(a) 
A fan

(b) 
A plant

(c) 
A toys

(d) 
A sponge

**33.** Which of the following food should be taken daily?

(a) 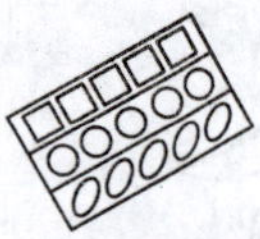
Sweets

(b) 
Chips

(c) 
Milk

(d) 
Noodles

**34.** Which is not true about the Sun?

(a) It gives us light

(b) It gives us heat

(c) It helps plants to make their food

(d) It can be seen at night

**35.** Match the animals given in Column I with the things we get from them in Column II.

| Column I | Column II |
|---|---|
| A.  | 1.  |
| B.  | 2.  |
| C.  | 3. 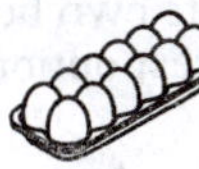 |

**Codes**

| | A | B | C | | A | B | C |
|---|---|---|---|---|---|---|---|
| (a) | 1 | 2 | 3 | (b) | 2 | 3 | 1 |
| (c) | 3 | 2 | 1 | (d) | 2 | 1 | 3 |

# Hints & Solutions

## Living and Non-living Things

1. (*c*) Ball is a non-living thing because it cannot grow, whereas tree, hen and cat can grow and hence, they are living things.
2. (*c*) Child is living thing because he can move on their own, whereas sharpener, computer and car cannot move on their own.
3. (*a*) Living things need food to grow. Here cow eats grass as food. Hence, cow is a living thing.
4. (*a*) Plants are living things. They can grow. Whereas ball, book and toy (horse) are non-living things.
5. (*c*) Option (c) shows bird with their young ones. This picture shows living things reproduce babies.
6. (*b*) Fan belongs to non-living things, while rest options are belong to living things.
7. (*d*) Camel can move on its own because camel is a living thing. Rest options are non-living things.
8. (*b*) Fish and ant are living, things, whereas kite, pen and aeroplane are non-living things.
9. (*c*) Living things can grow and move. Non-living things cannot move on their own and do not need food.
10. (*d*) Lamp is a non-living thing. Non-living thing cannot move on their own.
11. (*c*) Book is a non-living thing, but bird is a living thing. Because we know non-living things cannot move and breathe and living things can move and breathe.
12. (*a*) Among the given options tree has life while road, car, jeep doesn't have life.
13. (*c*) Living things need air, water and food to live and to grow.
14. (*c*) Rat takes air inside and exhales air. This action of rat shows that living things breathe.
15. (*d*) In the following picture, a baby child grow into an adult. This shows living things can grow.
16. (*a*) Tree is a living thing, while rest options are of non-living things.
17. (*c*) Mango tree should be placed under living thing heading.
18. (*a*) All living things need air, water and food to live and to grow.
19. (*d*) Fish is a living thing which lives in water, whereas other options lives on lands.
20. (*b*) (A) Peacock is living thing.
    (B) Box is a non-living thing.
    (C) Living things can move on their own.
21. (*a*) Things which are present in nature are called natural things. Plant is the natural living thing because its needs air and water to grow.
22. (*b*) Plant, bear, cow and cat are living thing. Hence, option (b) is incorrect statement.
23. (*d*) Plant is a living things which cannot move from one place to another, plants only show movement on its place.
24. (*b*) Drum, shoes, moon, telephone and house are non-living things, while cow, frog, man and bird are living thing.
25. (*c*) Statement in option (c) is incorrect because cycle is non-living thing, it cannot move on its own. It can move by the help of a boy.
26. (*b*) Plant is a living thing. It cannot live without food. Plants make their food on its own.

## Plants

1. (*d*) In the given figure point *A* shows flower part of plant and point *B* show fruit part of the plant.
2. (*a*) Fruit is formed in point *B*.
3. (*c*) Very big plants with wooden stems are called trees like mango tree.
4. (*c*) Apple is a fruit. Rest options are vegetables which we get from plants.
5. (*d*) Given figure shows seed of mango tree.
6. (*b*) Radish is a vegetable, while all others are flowers. It is the coloured part of plant.
7. (*b*) Grains which are eaten by us are called food grains. We get grains from herbs plants sugarcane is a shrub plant.
8. (*d*) Plants require air, water and sunlight for their growth. Without any one of them plant cannot grow.
9. (*a*) Tea plant is a shrub, tea leaves are used to make tea.

**10.** (*c*) *A* labelled part is root. Root holds the plant in the soil and it is present under the ground.

**11.** (*a*) *B* labelled part is stem. On stem, leaves, fruits and flowers are grown.

**12.** (*d*) *C* labelled part is leaves. Leaves are also known as kitchen of the plant because it makes food for the plant.

**13.** (*c*) Watermelon grows along the ground. Hence, it is a creeper. Rest options are grown on trees.

**14.** (*b*) All these seeds are get from fruits, they are also known as dry fruits.

**15.** (*d*) Mango has one seed in it and papaya has many seeds in it.

**16.** (*d*) Flowers, root, stem, leaves, fruits and seeds are parts of plant. Soil is not a part of plant.

**17.** (*c*) Flowers may be of many different colours like red, pink, orange, etc.

**18.** (*d*) Groundnut is not a spice. The true statement is groundnut is a dry fruit.

**19.** (*d*) Option (d) is incorrectly matched because we get wheat grains from wheat plant. Wheat grains are used to make chapatis.

**20.** (*c*) Coconut gives us oil. Rest options cannot gives us oil. They are only used as food.

**21.** (*b*) Given fruit is papaya and option (b) is shown the papaya tree.

**22.** (*d*) We get cereals, pulses, fruits, vegetables, etc. from plants. Some plants give fibres to make clothes like cotton. We do not get plastic from plants.

**23.** (*c*) The seeds of some plants like beans, grams, etc. are called pulses. These are eaten by us.

**24.** (*a*) The leaf of plant is banana tree, and this plant give banana fruit.

**25.** (*b*) Lotus is water plant. Plants that grow in or underwater are called as water plant.

**26** (*c*) In this box these are 5 vegetables, i.e. Pumpkin, potato, brinjal, ladyfinger and cucumber and 3 fruits, i.e. Apple, guava and orange and 1 flower, i.e. Lotus.

## Animals

**1.** (*c*) Wild animal lives in forests.

**2.** (*d*) Sheep is a domestic animal. It gives us wool.

**3.** (*a*) Lion lives in a forest. It is a wild animal, whereas buffalo, goat and dog are pet/domestic animal.

**4.** (*d*) Whale is the largest animal in the world. Elephant is the largest land animal.

**5.** (*c*) Rat is not a water animal. It is a land animal whereas crocodile, fish and tortoise are water animal.

**6.** (*c*) Insect have six legs and are small in size. Lizard is not an insect.

**7.** (*a*) We can see camels in desert mostly. They can easily walk on sand.

**8.** (*c*) Most birds build a nest on trees to live. Squirrel is not a bird. Hence, squirrel does not build a nest.

**9.** (*a*) Monkeys live on trees while donkey and elephant live on land and fishes live in water.

**10.** (*d*) Cow likes to eat grass.

**11.** (*b*) Animals like lion and tiger always eat flesh.

**12.** (*b*) Animals which live in farms are called as farm animals, e.g. ox, goat, horse, hen, etc.

**13.** (*b*) All of them have wings and feathers to fly but ostrich cannot fly.

**14.** (*d*) Ostrich, kiwi and penguin has feathers but they cannot fly.

**15.** (*c*) (a) Bird lives in nest.
(b) Honeybee lives in beehive.
(c) Horse lives in stable.
(d) Mouse lives in hole.

**16.** (*c*) Horse is an animal who lives in stable.

**17.** (*a*) Lions kill other animals for their food, they eat other animal flesh.

**18.** (*b*) Insects have six legs and one or more wings. Some insects had no wings like earthworm, ant, etc.
Birds have two legs, two feathers and one beak without teeth.

**19.** (*c*) Deer eats only plants. Its correct match is Bear-both plants and flesh.

**20.** (*c*) In fig *A* is horse, *B* - is mosquito and C is frog. Among them, mosquito is smallest then frog and then horse is a big animal, so increasing order is B < C < A.

**21.** (*b*) Snake has no hands or legs. It only crawls on land.

**22.** (*a*) Duck and swan can easily swim in water.

**23.** (*d*) Animal with tall neck is giraffe only.

24. (*a*) Hen lays eggs while cow, buffalo and lion do not lay eggs.

25. (*b*) Deer does not gives us milk. We get milk from cows, goats, buffaloes, etc.

## Human Beings

1. (*d*) Human body has 5 sense organs namely eyes, ears, nose, skin and tongue.
2. (*c*) We see a cartoon by our eyes, because eyes help us to see.
3. (*d*) We smell with the help of nose.
4. (*b*) Skin tells us that the tea is hot because skin help us to feel.
5. (*b*) While listening to music, we are using our ear because ears help us to hear.
6. (*a*) Teeth are used to cut and chew the food.
7. (*c*) Leg, knee and eblows help us to move and lift things. Eyes helps us to see thing.
8. (*b*) Bitter coffee is tasted by our tongue. Our tongue help us to sense the taste of our food.
9. (*a*) Nails are part of our fingers.
10. (*d*) Skin helps us to feel sensations such as warmth, cold, itching and pain. Hence, skin is the sense orgain by which we sense hot and cold.
11. (*c*) We can play carrom with the help of our hands and eyes. Eyes helps us to see the target, while hands help us to strike it.
12. (*a*) (A) Eyes helps us to read.
(B) Nose helps us to smell.
(C) Ear helps us to hear.
(D) Tongue helps us to taste.
13. (*c*) Body parts like hands, ears, eyes and legs are two in numbers present in our body.
14. (*b*) To carry school bag, we use shoulder.
15. (*c*) Jump is not the part of sense. See, hear and smell all are senses.
16. (*c*) We have five sense organs namely eyes, ears, nose, tongue and skin. Hair is not a part of sense organ.
17. (*a*) When we eat food, it goes to the stomach. In stomach, eaten food gets digested.
18. (*b*) Smell is not the function of skin. Its a function of nose.
19. (*a*) There are 10 fingers in our hands including thumb.
20. (*b*) Ear does not helps us to smell perfume. It is incorrectly matched. To smell perfume nose will helps us, while rest options are correctly matched with their function.
21. (*d*) The boy in the picture is having electric shock, so he represents the sense of touch.
22. (*d*) The item is spectacles which help us to see thing and it is used for eyes.
23. (*a*) Walking can be done by using legs. Eating can be done by using mouth and hands. Reading can be done by using eyes. Combing can be done by using hands.
24. (*c*) Part *P* is ear which helps us to hear.
Part *Q* is hand which helps us to hold things.
Part *R* is stomach which helps us to digest food.
Part *S* is leg which helps us in walking.
25. (*b*) Two little eyes to look around.
Two little **ears** to hear each sound.
One little **nose** to smell what's sweets.
One little **mouth** that likes to eat.
26. (*a*) We can taste food substances like burger, fruits etc., but we cannot taste television, pencil and kite.
27. (*c*) Hands will help us to write, clap, hold, etc.
28. (*a*) Raj's eyes has been covered. He will not see the rainbow or anything else.

## Safety Rules and First Aid

1. (*b*) Black is not a colour of traffic light. Traffic light contains only three colour that is red, yellow and green.
2. (*d*) Getting up late in the morning is not a good habit.
3. (*b*) Playing with sharp objects can hurt you like nail cutter, knife etc. If you get hurt, tell your elders.
4. (*d*) Plucking flowers and leaves is a bad habit.
5. (*a*) Electric switches should not be touched with wet hands. If you touch you may get electric shock.
6. (*c*) We should not play with sharp toys it may hurt you.
7. (*c*) Red light means stop.
Yellow light means ready to move.
Green light means move.
8. (*a*) You have to say sorry, when you pushed someone by mistake.
9. (*c*) Walking slowly on stairs are correct match. Rest matches can be corrected as
(a) Playing football in playground.
(b) Do not stand on desk.
(d) Bathing in the bathroom.

10. (*d*) While play, in playground we have to follow all the saftey rules like play with friends, waiting for your turn and do not push anyone on the swings.
11. (*b*) Put things in a first aid box, which helps to give the treatment like band-aid, dettol, scissors, cotton roll, etc.
12. (*a*) Option (a) shows zebra crossing, always use zebra crossing to cross the road.
13. (*a*) While travelling in a bus, getting into the bus in a line.
14. (*a*) A. Always wear seat belt in the car.
B. If you are a learner, always use swimming tube in the swimming pool.
C. Always wear helmet while riding the bike.
15. (*b*) Knife, blade and scissors are sharp objects. We should not play with them.

(*c*) Always walk on the footpath. Do not play on road.

17. (*b*) When light turns red, you can cross the road from zebra crossing.
18. (*c*) A red signal light means stop. A right turn can be made against a red light only after you stop and yield to pedestrains and vehicles in your path.
19. (*a*) The man who give instructions on the road is traffic police.
20. (*d*) Statement III is false. The true statement is never jump from a moving bus.
21. (*a*) Children should always go into the swimming pool with their coach, teacher or elder.
22. (*b*) Touching electrical switches, should not be done by the children because it may hurt children.
23. (*d*) Going when the green light appears, is a correct safety rule.
24. (*c*) First aid is the first medical help. If some one gets injured, first aid is given.
25. (*a*) We should cross the road when the traffic light is red because when the traffic light is red all the vehicles are stop.
26. (*d*) Sign of No Parking zone in P cut in a circle.

## Air, Water and Weather

1. (*b*) Air connot be seen. We can feel only, when it moves.
2. (*a*) Living things need air to breathe. Car is non-living thing.
3. (*c*) Air is colourless, tastless. It has weight and fills space.
4. (*b*) Moving air is called wind.
5. (*d*) (A) Plants need air to breathe.
(B) Clothes need air to dry.
(C) Birds need air to breathe and fly.
6. (*a*) In option (a) the day is rainy.
In option (b) the day is cloudy and sunny.
In option (c) the day is hot and sunny.
In option (d) the day is snowy and cold.
7. (*d*) For sleeping, water is not needed, while watering the plants, bathing and cleaning the floor water is needed.
8. (*d*) Rain is the main source of water on the Earth. Rainwater fills the rivers, pond, lake oceans, etc.
9. (*b*) Football and airtubes can be filled with air. Air gives shape to them.
10. (*a*) We can store water in bottles, bucket, tank, earthenpots, etc. A large amount of water can be stored in bigger containers. Hence, a water tank can store maximum quantity of water.
11. (*d*) Water is colourless and tasteless. Water takes up the shape in which they filled.
12. (*c*) In winter season, days are very cold.
13. (*c*) Swamp water is dirty and polluted. We should always avoid to drink dirty and polluted water because it can cause us serious disease and illness, e.g. Diarrhoea.
14. (*b*) Travelling in car (vehicle), causes air pollution and makes air dirty.
15. (*b*) In a picture girl has umbrella, it shows that day is rainy.
16. (*c*) If we drink dirty water, we may get sick. Always drink clean water, we can clean water by boiling or by using water purifier.
17. (*c*) In figure 'A' there is a Sun means the day is sunny.
In figure 'B' there is only clouds means the day is cloudy.
In figure 'C' there is a rainycloud means the day is rainy.
In figure 'D' there is wind blown means the day is windy.
18. (*c*) According to the weather report, Tuesday is windy because in the report, the leaves are falling.
19. (*a*) According to the weather report, Thursday is the hottest day because Sun shows the hot day.
20. (*d*) Sewage from factories makes river water polluted. Rest activities does not make water polluted.

## Our Universe

**1.** (*d*) We can see the Sun, the Moon and stars in the sky. But, we do not see the planets in the sky with our naked eyes.

**2.** (*c*) The Sun is spherical or round in shape.

**3.** (*b*) Statement (b) is incorrect because Sun is not a planet, it is a star.

**4.** (*c*) The Sun always rises from East direction.

**5.** (*a*) Very big and bright ball of fire in the sky is known as Sun.

**6.** (*d*) The Sun always rises from East and sets in the West.

**7.** (*d*) We can see Moon and stars at night, while Sun can be seen during the day.

**8.** (*b*) Moon can be seen in a different shape every night.

**9.** (*a*) There are eight planets in the solar system namely Mercury, Venus, Earth, Mars, Jupiter, Saturn, Uranus and Neptune.

**10.** (*a*) The Sun is a star.

**11.** (*a*) Moon never takes square shape.

**12.** (*c*) Rocket can take us to the Moon. A person travels in rocket is called astrounauts.

**13.** (*d*) There are so many stars present in the sky. We cannot count them.

**14.** (*c*) We see stars in the shape  .

**15.** (*b*) Earth is the only planet where life can exist.

**16.** (*b*) Sun is the closest star to the Earth.

**17.** (*a*) Moon can be seen at night, in morning we can see Sun.

**18.** (*b*) Earth is the only planet while Sun is a star and Moon is a natural satellite.

**19.** (*a*) Moon is a natural satellite which revolves around the Earth.

## Practice Set 1

**1.** (*d*) Penguin does not live in forest. It lives in colder region.

**2.** (*d*) The shape of the gibbous Moon is

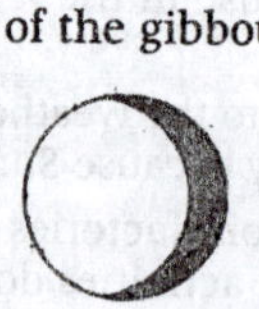

**3.** (*a*) Headphones is kept on the ears. Ears help us to hear the songs.

**4.** (*c*) Mango and litchi have one seed in it. Watermelon has many seeds in it. Apple has four seeds in it.

**5.** (*b*) (A) Figure 'A' shows brushing teeth.
(B) Figure 'B' shows washing hands.
(C) Figure 'C' shows cutting nails.
(D) Figure 'D' shows doing exercise.

**6.** (*b*) Elephant and *Cactus* both are living things but only elephant needs to move in search of food. *Cactus* makes their own food.

**7.** (*c*) Air is need to fill such items like balloon, football, swimming tube, tyre, cycle tubes, etc.

**8.** (*b*) In the given figure, Ankit is playing videogame. He used eyes to watch videogame, ears to hear the sound of videogame and hands to play the videogame.

**9.** (*d*) (A) Watermelon is a creeper.
(B) Rose plant is a shrub.
(C) Pea plant is a climber.
(D) Coriander plant is a herb.

**10.** (*b*) Both 1 and 2 statements are correct reason for keeping the rivers clean because if we drink dirty water of river it may cause diseases.

**11.** (*a*) Only statement 2 is true. Rest true statements are
1. Tiger eats flesh of other animals.
2. Wild animals live in the forest.

**12.** (*a*)

 represents zebra crossing.

 represents men at work.

 represents school ahead.

 represents hospital ahead.

**13.** (*c*) The Sun, the Moon and stars are seen in the sky. They all are far from us.

**14.** (*c*) Teddy bear is a non-living thing and puppy is a living thing. Only living thing will grow.

**15.** (*c*) We should drink pure water only. To make water pure, firstly boils it. Drinking impure water can cause many diseases and makes us ill.

**16.** (*a*) The outer covering of teeth is of white substance. So, the colour of the teeth is white.

**17.** (*b*) Neem and tulsi plants are used in making medicines. So, these plants also called as medicinal plants.

**18.** (*b*) The shape of the planet Earth and others planet is like a circle or oval.

**19.** (*c*) First aid box contains scissors, painkiller tablets, band-aid, cotton roll, etc. Matchstick is not found in first aid box.

**20.** (*d*) (A) Squirrels eats nuts, seeds, etc.
(B) Giraffe eats grass.
(C) Elephant eats sugarcane.

**21.** (*a*) In option (a) fish is living and bowl is non-living.
In option (b) Pencil and pencil box both are non-living.
In option (c) birds and tree both are living.
In option (d) water and bottle both are non-living.

**22.** (*c*) Only option (c) is true. Rest options can be corrected as
(a) Air has no colour.
(b) Air has no taste.
(d) Air present everywhere.

**23.** (*d*) We get butter from cows or buffaloes milk and honey from honeybees. Hence, they are animal products. We make idli from riceflour, juice from fruits and bread from wheat flour. Hence, they are plant products.

**24.** (*c*) (A) Using swimming tube, while swimming.
(B) Using helmet while cycling.
(C) Using zebra crossing for crossing the road.
(D) Wearing seat belt while driving.
All are safety rules to avoid accidents.

**25.** (*c*) *M* is shed leaves. Shed leaves are not part of tree anymore. Hence, it is non-living thing. *N* is bench. It is also non-living thing.

**26.** (*d*) Eyes and ears are the part of the head. Knee is the part of the leg and elbow is the part of the hand.

**27.** (*a*) We can see only Sun during the day. Stars and the Moon can be seen at night, while we cannot see the planets with our naked eyes.

**28.** (*d*) Statement in option (d) is incorrect because parrot and pigeon can fly but penguin cannot fly.

**29.** (*b*) Plant is living thing but cannot move from its place. It shows movement at their place only.

**30.** (*d*) Cow, buffalo and goat, all animals give us milk.

**31.** (*a*) Walking on footpath is one of the safety rules. Running on road, playing with sharp objects and touch electric switches with wet hands are not safety rules. You may get hurt in such activities.

**32.** (*d*) So many stars are present in the sky. You cannot count them.

**33.** (*a*) In the given figure
*P* is bud - give rise to flower
*Q* is stem - supply food and water to plant parts
*R* is leaf - prepare food for plant
*S* is fruit - contains seed in it.

**34.** (*d*) Wrist is not a part of leg. It is a part of our hand.

**35.** (*c*) Statement I is incorrect. It can be corrected as air and water are non-living things.

## Practice Set 2

**1.** (*d*) Butterfly is living thing, while jeep, bus and fan are non-living thing.

**2.** (*a*) The animal shown in a picture is cow, and cow lives in shed.

**3.** (*c*) Toy and book are safe to play, while scissors and knife are not safe to play. They are sharp objects, you may get hurt from them.

**4.** (*a*) All planets move around the Sun. Sun gives heat and light to the planets.

**5.** (*b*) Option (b) is incorrectly matched. The correct match of watermelon is with creeper.

**6.** (*c*) We have 2 eyes. Eyes help us to see the world.

**7.** (*c*) Boiling of water can make water pure and germ free. This water is safe to drink.

**8.** (*c*) All are insects. Bee, mosquito and butterfly can fly but ant cannot fly.

**9.** (*b*) We can count Sun, Moon and planet on fingers they are 1, 1 and 8 respectively in numbers. We cannot count stars as they are so many in the sky.

**10.** (*b*) To hold the racket, the boy used the hands. Hands also help us to write.

**11.** (*b*) Statement I is incorrect because plant is living thing but it cannot move by itself. It only shows movement at their place.

**12.** (*d*) In figure A, boy is playing with electric switch.
In figure B, boy is playing on road.
In figure C, boy is playing with fire.
They all are not following safety rules.

**13.** (*d*) Labelled part are as follows
A - Leaf B - Fruit
C - Flower D - Bud
A - leaf is known as the 'kitchen of the plant' as it makes food for the plant.

**14.** (*a*) The boy needs air to flying the kite. Air helps us in many ways.

**15.** (*a*) (A) Eyes help us to read book
(B) Nose helps us to smell
(C) Ears help us to hear
(D) Tongue helps us to taste

**16.** (*a*) The correct sequence is $B \to D \to A \to C$

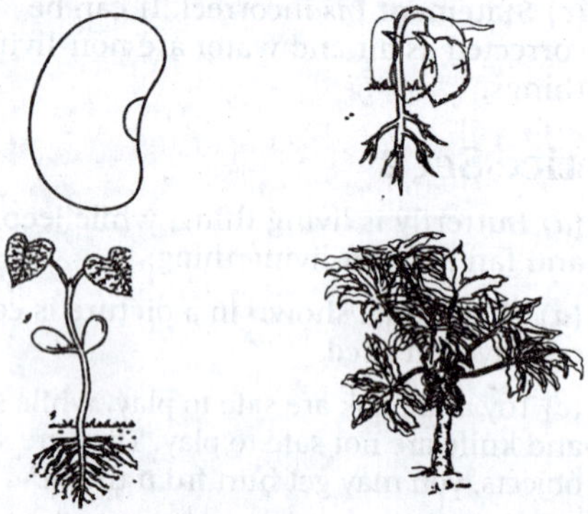

**17.** (*c*) Raincoats, umbrella and gumboots are used in rainy season. This season is also known as monsoon.

**18.** (*c*) The given picture shows the spider web. It is a home of spider.

**19.** (*c*) Activities shown in figure 'a', 'b' and 'd' are not following safety rules. Figure 'c' is following safety rule.

**20.** (*b*) Moon moves around the Earth. It is a natural satellite on the Earth.

**21.** (*a*) All living things need air, water and food to live and grow. Plants need sunlight also.

**22.** (*c*) Sweaters, woolen socks and caps, jackets and coats are required in winter season. These items keep us warm.

**23.** (*a*) (A) Mustard oil is obtained from mustard seeds.
(B) Flower of cotton plant is used to make cotton shirt.
(C) Trunk of tree is used to making furnitures like chair, table, etc.

**24.** (*d*) While reading a letter, Raghav used his eyes. Eyes help us to see the things.

**25.** (*a*) Sun rises in the East and sets in the West. So, the direction of Raju's window is in the East.

**26.** (*a*) First aid means the first treatment given to a patient before the doctor arrives.

**27.** (*c*) Both statements I and II are correct. All animals do not give us milk. Some give us egg like hen, meat like goat and hen, etc.

**28.** (*b*) Bird is wrongly placed under non-living things. Bird should be placed under living things.

**29.** (*b*) Water in the freezer change into the ice after some time.

**30.** (*d*) In the given figure, pulses are placed in every container.

**31.** (*c*) While crossing the road, one should not be running, talking on the mobile, listening to music. If these things you and do on the road, you may have the accident.

**32.** (*b*) Plant is a living thing, it can grow after some days. In some years, it changes into tree.

**33.** (*c*) Milk is a healthy food. It should be taken daily for body health. Sweets, chips and noodles are not taken daily.

**34.** (*d*) Sun cannot be seen at night. It only can seen during the day.

**35.** (*b*) (A) Goat gives us milk.
(B) Hen gives us egg and meat
(C) Sheep gives us wool.